CONTENTS

8

21

37

It's Better with Butter

Nothing equals the wonderful flavor of real butter and the homemade goodness it adds to baked goods. When you bake, butter plays a major role in tenderizing, adding flavor and color, and helping baked goods to brown. Here are some tips for better baking with butter:

What is the best way to soften butter? Soften butter for easier mixing by removing it from the refrigerator and letting it stand 30 to 45 minutes at room temperature. In a hurry? Cut butter into chunks and let it stand 15 minutes at room temperature, or place a stick of cold butter between sheets of waxed paper and smash it on both sides with a rolling pin. We don't recommend softening butter in the microwave because it can melt too quickly.

Can salted and unsalted butter be substituted for one another? Salted and unsalted butter may be substituted for one another without altering the amount of salt in the recipe. Unsalted butter gives recipes a delicate, cultured flavor.

How long can I store my butter? It is recommended that butter be used by the code date on the package to ensure quality. For longer storage, place the carton in a resealable plastic food storage bag or wrap in aluminum foil and freeze for up to four months from the time of purchase.

MEASURING TIPS

Cut sticks as marked on the wrapper, using a sharp knife.

Cup	Equivalent Measure(s)
1 cup	2 sticks or ½ pound
⅔ cup	10 tablespoons plus 2 teaspoons
½ cup	1 stick or ¼ pound
⅓ cup	5 tablespoons plus 1 teaspoon
¼ cup	½ stick or 4 tablespoons

Chocolate Caramel Shortbread Fingers

Preparation time: **20 minutes** | Baking time: **22 minutes** | **30 cookies**

COOKIE

- ½ cup **LAND O LAKES®** Butter, softened
- ¼ cup powdered sugar
- 2 tablespoons firmly packed brown sugar
- 1¼ cups all-purpose flour
- ¾ teaspoon baking powder
- ¼ teaspoon salt

TOPPING

- ⅓ cup caramel ice cream topping
- ¼ cup slivered almonds, coarsely chopped
- 2 ounces milk chocolate, chopped

• Heat oven to 325°F. Line 8-inch square baking pan with aluminum foil leaving a 1-inch overhang.

• Combine butter, powdered sugar and brown sugar in large bowl. Beat at medium speed, scraping bowl often, until creamy. Reduce speed to low; add flour, baking powder and salt. Beat until well mixed.

• Press dough into prepared pan; prick with fork every ½ inch. Bake for 22 to 25 minutes or until lightly browned. Lift cookies from pan using aluminum foil. Place on cutting board. Immediately cut into 30 (2¾×¾-inch) pieces.

• Place caramel topping in small saucepan. Cook over medium heat, stirring constantly, until caramel has slightly thickened (2 to 3 minutes). Remove from heat; drizzle caramel over cookies. Sprinkle with almonds. Cool to lukewarm; carefully separate. Cool completely.

• Melt chocolate in small microwave-safe dish on MEDIUM (50% power) until soft (1 to 1½ minutes). Stir until smooth. Drizzle over cooled cookies. Let stand until set.

Chinese Almond Cookies

Preparation time: **40 minutes** | Baking time: **11 minutes per pan** | **4 dozen cookies**

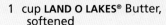

1	cup **LAND O LAKES®** Butter, softened	1	teaspoon baking powder
¾	cup sugar	¼	teaspoon salt
1	egg	48	whole blanched almonds
1	teaspoon almond extract	1	egg yolk
2¼	cups all-purpose flour	1	tablespoon water

• Heat oven to 350°F. Combine butter and sugar in large bowl. Beat at medium speed, scraping bowl often, until creamy. Add egg and almond extract; beat until well mixed. Reduce speed to low; add flour, baking powder and salt. Beat until well mixed.

• Shape dough into 1¼-inch balls. Place 2 inches apart onto ungreased cookie sheet. Flatten slightly; press almond into center of each cookie.

• Beat egg yolk with water in small bowl; brush cookies with egg mixture. Bake for 11 to 15 minutes or until just set.

PB & Jam Bites

Preparation time: **20 minutes** | **32 bars**

BAR

- 3 cups miniature marshmallows
- 1 cup crunchy peanut butter
- ½ cup **LAND O LAKES®** Butter
- 4½ cups crisp rice cereal

FILLING

- ⅔ cup strawberry, apricot or peach jam

TOPPING

- ½ cup milk chocolate chips
- 1 tablespoon crunchy peanut butter
- 2 teaspoons shortening

• Melt marshmallows, 1 cup peanut butter and butter in 3-quart saucepan over low heat, stirring constantly, until smooth (4 to 5 minutes). Add cereal; quickly stir until well coated. Press mixture into ungreased 11×7-inch pan.

• Spoon jam by teaspoonfuls over hot cereal mixture; gently spread over top.

• Melt chocolate chips, 1 tablespoon peanut butter and shortening in 1-quart saucepan over low heat, stirring occasionally, until smooth (2 to 4 minutes). Gently spread over jam layer. Refrigerate until chocolate layer is firm (about 2 hours). Cut into bars.

Best Ever Butter Cookies

Preparation time: 40 minutes | Baking time: **6 minutes per pan** | **3 dozen cookies**

COOKIE

- 1 cup **LAND O LAKES®** Butter, softened
- 1 cup sugar
- 1 egg
- 2 tablespoons orange juice
- 1 tablespoon vanilla
- 2½ cups all-purpose flour
- 1 teaspoon baking powder

FROSTING

- 3 cups powdered sugar
- ⅓ cup **LAND O LAKES®** Butter, softened
- 1 teaspoon vanilla
- 1 to 2 tablespoons milk
  Food color, if desired

  Decorator candies and/or sugars, if desired

• Combine 1 cup butter, sugar and egg in large bowl. Beat at medium speed, scraping bowl often, until creamy. Add orange juice and 1 tablespoon vanilla; mix well. Reduce speed to low; add flour and baking powder. Beat until well mixed.

• Divide dough into thirds; wrap each in plastic food wrap. Refrigerate until firm (2 to 3 hours).

• Heat oven to 400°F. Roll out dough on lightly floured surface, one-third at a time (keeping remaining dough refrigerated), to ⅛- to ¼-inch thickness. Cut with 3-inch cookie cutters. Place 1 inch apart onto ungreased cookie sheets. Bake for 6 to 10 minutes or until edges are lightly browned. Cool completely.

• Combine powdered sugar, ⅓ cup butter and 1 teaspoon vanilla in small bowl. Beat at low speed, scraping bowl often and adding enough milk for desired spreading consistency. Tint frosting with food color, if desired. Frost and decorate cooled cookies as desired.

Chocolate Pixies

Preparation time: **30 minutes** | Baking time: **15 minutes** per pan | **4 dozen cookies**

¼ cup **LAND O LAKES®** Butter
4 (1-ounce) squares unsweetened baking chocolate
2 cups all-purpose flour
2 cups sugar
4 eggs

2 teaspoons baking powder
½ teaspoon salt
½ cup chopped walnuts *or* pecans

Powdered sugar

• Melt butter and chocolate in 1-quart saucepan over low heat, stirring occasionally, until smooth (8 to 10 minutes). Cool completely (30 minutes).

• Combine melted chocolate mixture, 1 cup flour, sugar, eggs, baking powder and salt in large bowl. Beat at medium speed, scraping bowl often, until well mixed. Stir in remaining flour and nuts by hand. Cover; refrigerate until firm (2 hours).

• Heat oven to 300°F. Shape dough into 1½-inch balls. Roll in powdered sugar. Place 2 inches apart onto greased cookie sheets. Bake for 15 to 18 minutes or until set.

Glazed Apple Pie Bars

Preparation time: **1 hour** | Baking time: **45 minutes** | **36 bars**

PASTRY

- 1 egg, separated, reserve white
- ½ cup milk
- 2½ cups all-purpose flour
- 1 teaspoon salt
- 1 cup cold **LAND O LAKES®** Butter

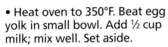

FILLING

- 1 cup crushed corn flakes
- 8 to 10 medium (8 cups) tart cooking apples, peeled, sliced

- 1 cup sugar
- 2 teaspoons ground cinnamon
- ½ teaspoon ground nutmeg
- 1 reserved egg white
- 2 tablespoons sugar

GLAZE

- 1 cup powdered sugar
- ½ teaspoon vanilla
- 1 to 2 tablespoons milk

• Heat oven to 350°F. Beat egg yolk in small bowl. Add ½ cup milk; mix well. Set aside.

• Combine flour and salt in medium bowl; cut in butter with pastry blender or fork until mixture resembles coarse crumbs. Stir in egg yolk mixture with fork until dough forms a ball. Divide dough in half.

• Roll out half of dough on lightly floured surface into 15×10-inch rectangle; place onto bottom of ungreased 15×10×1-inch jelly-roll pan. Sprinkle with corn flakes; top with apples.

• Combine 1 cup sugar, 1½ teaspoons cinnamon and nutmeg in small bowl. Sprinkle over apples. Roll remaining half of dough into 15½×10½-inch rectangle; place over apples.

• Beat egg white with fork until foamy; brush over top crust. Combine remaining cinnamon and 2 tablespoons sugar in small bowl; sprinkle over crust. Bake for 45 to 60 minutes or until lightly browned.

• Combine powdered sugar, vanilla and enough milk for desired glazing consistency in small bowl. Drizzle over warm bars.

Cranberry Vanilla Chip Bars

Preparation time: **15 minutes** | Baking time: **25 minutes** | 16 bars

BAR

- ½ cup sugar
- ⅓ cup **LAND O LAKES®** Butter, softened
- ¼ cup firmly packed brown sugar
- 1 egg
- 1 teaspoon vanilla
- 1 cup all-purpose flour
- ½ teaspoon baking powder
- ¼ teaspoon salt
- ½ cup sweetened dried cranberries
- ½ cup white baking chips
- ½ cup chopped pecans, if desired

GLAZE

- ¼ cup white baking chips
- ½ teaspoon shortening

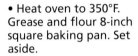

- Heat oven to 350°F. Grease and flour 8-inch square baking pan. Set aside.

- Combine sugar, butter, brown sugar, egg and vanilla in large bowl. Beat at medium speed, scraping bowl often, until well mixed. Reduce speed to low; add flour, baking powder and salt. Beat until well mixed. Stir in cranberries, ½ cup white baking chips and pecans by hand.

- Spread batter into prepared pan. Bake for 25 to 30 minutes or until toothpick inserted in center comes out clean. Cool completely.

- Melt ¼ cup white baking chips and shortening in 1-quart saucepan over low heat, stirring constantly, until smooth. Drizzle over cooled bars. Cut into bars.

Double Chip Pecan Cookies

Preparation time: **45 minutes** | Baking time: **9 minutes per pan** | **4½ dozen cookies**

1 cup **LAND O LAKES®** Butter, softened
¾ cup sugar
¾ cup firmly packed brown sugar
2 eggs
1 teaspoon vanilla
2¼ cups all-purpose flour

1 teaspoon baking soda
½ teaspoon salt
½ cup chopped pecans
1 (12-ounce) package (2 cups) real semi-sweet chocolate chips
1 cup butterscotch-flavored chips*

• Heat oven to 375°F. Combine butter, sugar, brown sugar, eggs and vanilla in large bowl. Beat at medium speed, scraping bowl often, until creamy. Reduce speed to low; add flour, baking soda and salt. Beat until well mixed. Stir in pecans, chocolate chips and butterscotch chips by hand.

• Drop dough by rounded teaspoonfuls, 2 inches apart, onto lightly greased cookie sheets. Bake for 9 to 12 minutes or until lightly browned. Cool 1 minute; remove from cookie sheet.

*Substitute 1 cup (6 ounces) coarsely chopped white chocolate.

Fudgy Raspberry Brownies

Preparation time: **15 minutes** | Baking time: **40 minutes** | **36 brownies**

BROWNIE

- 1 cup **LAND O LAKES®** Butter
- 4 (1-ounce) squares unsweetened baking chocolate
- 2 cups sugar
- 4 eggs
- 1 teaspoon vanilla
- 1 teaspoon almond extract

- 1½ cups all-purpose flour
- ¼ teaspoon salt
- ½ cup seedless raspberry jam

GLAZE

- ¼ cup **LAND O LAKES™** Heavy Whipping Cream
- 4 (1-ounce) squares semi-sweet baking chocolate

• Heat oven to 350°F. Place butter and unsweetened chocolate in medium microwave-safe bowl. Microwave on HIGH for 1 minute; stir. Microwave 30 seconds; stir until smooth. Set aside.

• Combine sugar, eggs, vanilla and almond extract in large bowl. Beat at medium speed, until well mixed. Add melted chocolate mixture; continue beating until well mixed. Reduce speed to low; add flour and salt. Beat just until mixed. Spread batter into greased 13×9-inch baking pan.

• Stir jam until smooth. Drop tablespoonfuls of jam evenly over batter. Swirl jam through batter using knife. Bake for 40 to 45 minutes or until set and brownies begin to pull away from sides of pan. (DO NOT OVERBAKE.) Cool completely.

• Place whipping cream in 1-quart saucepan. Cook over medium heat just until cream begins to boil (1 to 2 minutes). Add semi-sweet chocolate; remove from heat. Stir with wire whisk until smooth. Spread over brownies.

tip:

For easy pan removal and cutting, line baking pan with aluminum foil, leaving 1-inch overhang on ends; lightly grease foil. Once brownies are cooled and frosted, remove them by lifting foil at edges. Cut into bars.

Orange Buttercream Squares

Preparation time: 30 minutes | 25 bars

CRUST

1¼ cups (about 25) finely crushed chocolate wafer cookies
⅓ cup **LAND O LAKES®** Butter, softened

FILLING

1½ cups powdered sugar
⅓ cup **LAND O LAKES®** Butter, softened
1 tablespoon milk
2 teaspoons freshly grated orange peel
½ teaspoon vanilla

GLAZE

1 tablespoon **LAND O LAKES®** Butter, melted
1 tablespoon unsweetened cocoa

• Combine all crust ingredients in medium bowl. Press mixture onto bottom of ungreased 8-inch square pan. Cover; refrigerate until firm (1 hour).

• Combine all filling ingredients in small bowl. Beat at medium speed until creamy. Spread over crust.

• Combine all glaze ingredients in small bowl; drizzle over filling. Refrigerate until firm (1 to 2 hours). Cut into bars. Store, covered, in refrigerator.

Pecan Pie Cookies

Preparation time: **30 minutes** | Baking time: **8 minutes per pan** | **3 dozen cookies**

COOKIE

- 1 cup firmly packed brown sugar
- ¾ cup **LAND O LAKES®** Butter, softened
- 1 egg
- 1 teaspoon vanilla
- 2 cups all-purpose flour
- 1 teaspoon baking powder

FILLING

- 1 cup chopped pecans
- ½ cup firmly packed brown sugar
- ¼ cup **LAND O LAKES™** Heavy Whipping Cream
- 1 teaspoon vanilla

• Heat oven to 350°F. Combine all cookie ingredients except flour and baking powder in large bowl. Beat at medium speed until creamy. Reduce speed to low; add flour and baking powder. Beat until well mixed.

• Shape dough into 1¼-inch balls. Place 2 inches apart onto ungreased cookie sheets. Make indentation in each cookie with thumb; rotate thumb to hollow out slightly.

• Combine all filling ingredients in small bowl; fill each cookie with 1 rounded teaspoon filling. Bake for 8 to 12 minutes or until lightly browned. Cool 1 minute; remove from cookie sheets.

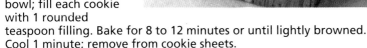

Peppermint 'n Chocolate Bars

Preparation time: **25 minutes** | **48 bars**

CRUST

- ¾ cup **LAND O LAKES®** Butter
- ½ cup sugar
- ⅓ cup unsweetened cocoa
- 1 teaspoon vanilla
- 2 cups graham cracker crumbs
- 1 cup sweetened flaked coconut
- ½ cup chopped nuts

FILLING

- 2 cups powdered sugar

- ½ cup **LAND O LAKES®** Butter, softened
- 2 tablespoons milk
- 1 teaspoon peppermint extract
- 3 drops green *or* red food color, if desired

GLAZE

- ⅓ cup real semi-sweet chocolate chips
- 1 teaspoon vegetable oil

• Combine ¾ cup butter, sugar, cocoa and vanilla in 2-quart saucepan. Cook over medium heat, stirring constantly, until butter is melted and mixture is smooth (1 to 2 minutes). Stir in all remaining crust ingredients. Press mixture firmly onto bottom of ungreased 13×9-inch baking pan. Refrigerate until firm (15 to 20 minutes).

• Combine all filling ingredients in small bowl. Beat at medium speed, scraping bowl often, until smooth. Spread filling evenly over crust; refrigerate 15 minutes.

• Melt chocolate chips and oil in 1-quart saucepan over low heat, stirring constantly, until smooth (2 to 4 minutes). Drizzle over bars. Cover; refrigerate until firm (2 to 3 hours). Cut into bars. Store refrigerated.

Raspberry Almond Shortbread Thumbprints

Preparation time: **45 minutes** | Baking time: **14 minutes per pan** | **3½ dozen cookies**

COOKIE
- 1 cup **LAND O LAKES®** Butter, softened
- ⅔ cup sugar
- ½ teaspoon almond extract
- 2 cups all-purpose flour
- ½ cup raspberry jam

GLAZE
- 1 cup powdered sugar
- 1½ teaspoons almond extract
- 2 to 3 teaspoons water

• Combine butter, sugar and ½ teaspoon almond extract in large bowl. Beat at medium speed, scraping bowl often, until creamy. Reduce speed to low; add flour. Beat until well mixed. Cover; refrigerate until firm (at least 1 hour).

• Heat oven to 350°F. Shape dough into 1-inch balls. Place 2 inches apart onto ungreased cookie sheets. Make indentation in center of each cookie with thumb (edges may crack slightly). Fill each indentation with about ¼ teaspoon jam.

• Bake for 14 to 18 minutes or until edges are lightly browned. Let stand 1 minute; remove from cookie sheets. Cool completely.

• Meanwhile, combine powdered sugar, 1½ teaspoons almond extract and enough water for desired glazing consistency in small bowl with wire whisk until smooth. Drizzle over cooled cookies.

Toasted Pecan Toffee Bars

Preparation time: **20 minutes** | Baking time: **25 minutes** | **36 bars**

BAR

2 cups all-purpose flour

1 cup **LAND O LAKES®** Butter, softened

1 cup firmly packed brown sugar

½ teaspoon ground cinnamon

1 teaspoon vanilla

¾ cup chopped pecans, toasted

½ cup milk chocolate chips

TOPPING

½ cup milk chocolate chips

¼ cup chopped pecans, toasted

• Heat oven to 350°F. Combine all bar ingredients except ¾ cup pecans and ½ cup milk chocolate chips in large bowl. Beat at low speed, scraping bowl often, until mixture resembles coarse crumbs. Stir in ¾ cup pecans and ½ cup milk chocolate chips by hand.

• Press mixture onto bottom of greased 13×9-inch baking pan. Bake for 25 to 30 minutes or until edges are lightly browned.

• Immediately sprinkle with ½ cup milk chocolate chips; let stand 5 minutes. Slightly swirl chips as they melt, leaving some whole for a marbled effect. Immediately sprinkle with ¼ cup pecans. Cool completely. Cut into bars.

Super Fudgy Three Way Topped Brownies

Preparation time: **20 minutes** | Baking time: **30 minutes** | **16 brownies**

¾ cup **LAND O LAKES®** Butter
⅔ cup sugar
1 (12-ounce) package (2 cups) real semi-sweet chocolate chips

2 eggs
½ teaspoon vanilla
1 cup all-purpose flour
½ teaspoon baking powder
⅛ teaspoon salt

• Heat oven to 350°F. Place butter and sugar in large microwave-safe bowl. Microwave on HIGH for 2 minutes or until mixture just starts to boil; stir until well mixed. Add 1 cup chocolate chips; stir until melted. Add eggs and vanilla; mix well. Add flour, baking powder and salt; mix well. Stir in remaining chocolate chips.

• Pour batter into ungreased 8-inch square baking pan. Bake for 30 to 35 minutes or until toothpick inserted in center comes out with moist crumbs. Top brownies as desired.

variations:

PEANUT BUTTER CUP BROWNIES: Prepare brownies as directed above. Meanwhile, coarsely chop 3 (1.5-ounce) packages unwrapped peanut butter cups. Sprinkle evenly over hot brownies. Lightly press into brownies. Cool completely before cutting.

S'MORE DESSERT BROWNIES: Prepare brownies as directed above. Cool completely. Just before serving, cut cooled brownies into 16 servings; place each bar onto individual serving plate. Dollop each with 1 tablespoon marshmallow crème; sprinkle with crushed graham crackers.

CANDY CARAMEL BROWNIES: Prepare brownies as directed above. Meanwhile, cut 2 (1.7-ounce) packages round chewy caramels in milk chocolate into fourths. Sprinkle evenly over hot brownies. Lightly press into brownies. Cool completely before cutting.

Crumb Top Rhubarb Pie

Preparation time: **40 minutes** | Baking time: **50 minutes** | 8 servings

CRUST
- 1 cup all-purpose flour
- ⅛ teaspoon salt
- ⅓ cup cold **LAND O LAKES®** Butter
- 3 to 4 tablespoons cold water

FILLING
- 1¼ cups sugar
- 3 tablespoons cornstarch
- ½ teaspoon ground cinnamon
- ¼ teaspoon ground nutmeg
- 4 cups sliced ¼-inch fresh rhubarb
- ⅔ cup chopped pecans

TOPPING
- 1 cup all-purpose flour
- ⅔ cup sugar
- ½ cup cold **LAND O LAKES®** Butter

• Heat oven to 400°F. Combine 1 cup flour and salt in large bowl; cut in ⅓ cup butter with pastry blender or fork until mixture resembles coarse crumbs. Stir in enough water with fork just until flour is moistened. Shape into ball; flatten slightly.

• Roll out ball of dough on lightly floured surface into 12-inch circle. Fold into quarters. Place dough into 9-inch deep-dish pie pan; unfold, pressing firmly against bottom and sides. Trim crust to ½ inch from edge of pan. Crimp or flute edge. Set aside.

• Combine all filling ingredients except rhubarb and pecans in large bowl. Add rhubarb; toss until well coated. Spoon into prepared crust; sprinkle with pecans. Set aside.

• Combine 1 cup flour and ⅔ cup sugar in medium bowl; cut in ½ cup butter with pastry blender or fork until mixture resembles coarse crumbs. Sprinkle mixture over rhubarb. Cover edge of crust with 2-inch strip of aluminum foil. Bake for 50 to 60 minutes or until topping is golden brown and filling bubbles around edges. Remove aluminum foil during last 10 minutes, if desired.

Fudgy Turtle Brownie Pie

Preparation time: **20 minutes** | Baking time: **33 minutes** | 8 servings

BROWNIE
- 1 (19.4-ounce) package brownie mix with pecans
- 3 tablespoons water
- ½ cup **LAND O LAKES®** Butter, melted
- 2 eggs
- 12 caramels, unwrapped, cut in half

SAUCE
- 15 caramels, unwrapped
- ⅓ cup real semi-sweet chocolate chips
- ¼ cup **LAND O LAKES™** Half & Half

TOPPING
- 1 quart butter pecan ice cream, softened
- ½ cup chopped pecans, if desired

• Heat oven to 350°F. Grease bottom only of 9-inch pie pan. Set aside.

• Combine all brownie ingredients except caramels in large bowl; stir until well mixed.

• Spread batter into prepared pan. Place caramel halves evenly over batter; press down lightly. Bake for 33 to 38 minutes or until top is set and toothpick inserted 2 inches from side comes out clean. Score into wedges while warm. Cool completely; cut into wedges.

• Meanwhile, combine all sauce ingredients in 1-quart saucepan. Cook over medium heat, stirring constantly, until smooth. Cool 5 minutes.

• To serve, place brownie wedges on individual serving plates. Top with ice cream; drizzle with sauce. Sprinkle with pecans, if desired.

tip:

Refrigerate any leftover sauce; reheat before serving.

Mini Pineapple Ginger Upside-Down Cakes

Preparation time: **20 minutes** | Baking time: **20 minutes** | **12 mini cakes**

TOPPING

- ½ cup firmly packed brown sugar
- 1 (8-ounce) can pineapple tidbits, well-drained
- 3 tablespoons **LAND O LAKES®** Butter, melted

CAKES

- 1⅓ cups all-purpose flour
- ½ cup firmly packed brown sugar
- 1 teaspoon baking powder
- 1 teaspoon ground ginger

- ½ teaspoon salt
- ¼ teaspoon baking soda
- ¼ cup **LAND O LAKES®** Butter, melted
- 1 (8-ounce) container plain yogurt
- 1 egg, beaten

LAND O LAKES™ Heavy Whipping Cream, whipped, if desired
Maraschino cherries, if desired

• Heat oven to 375°F. Combine all topping ingredients in small bowl. Place 1 tablespoon topping mixture into each greased 1¼-inch deep muffin cup.

• Combine flour, brown sugar, baking powder, ginger, salt and baking soda in large bowl. Add ¼ cup butter, yogurt and egg; mix well.

• Spoon batter over topping mixture in muffin cups. Bake for 20 to 25 minutes or until tops are golden brown. Cool 3 minutes. Immediately turn onto serving plate. Serve warm. Top with whipped cream and cherry, if desired.

Plum Crostata

Preparation time: **15 minutes** | Baking time: **40 minutes** | **10 servings**

CRUST

- 2 cups all-purpose flour
- ¼ cup sugar
- ½ teaspoon salt
- ¾ cup cold **LAND O LAKES®** Butter
- 6 to 8 tablespoons cold water

FILLING

- 6 medium (3 cups) ripe plums, pitted, sliced ⅛-inch thick
- ½ cup firmly packed brown sugar
- 1 tablespoon orange juice
- 1 to 2 teaspoons freshly grated orange peel

Powdered sugar, if desired

• Heat oven to 400°F. Combine flour, sugar and salt in medium bowl; cut in butter with pastry blender or fork until mixture resembles coarse crumbs. Mix in water with fork until flour is just moistened.

• Press or roll pastry into 14-inch circle onto ungreased baking sheet. Shape into 10-inch circle by forming 2-inch rim around outside edge; loosely crimp edge. Prick bottom of pastry with fork. Bake for 15 minutes.

• Arrange plums in pinwheel fashion on pastry. Stir together brown sugar, orange juice and orange peel in small bowl; spread evenly over plums. Continue baking for 25 to 30 minutes or until pastry is golden brown.

• Just before serving, sprinkle with powdered sugar, if desired.

Coconut-Banana Cake

Preparation time: **20 minutes** | Baking time: **30 minutes** | **16 servings**

CAKE
- 1 (18.25-ounce) package spice or carrot cake mix
- 1 cup water
- 1 large (⅔ cup) ripe banana, mashed
- 3 eggs
- ¾ cup sweetened flaked coconut

FROSTING
- 4 cups powdered sugar
- ½ cup **LAND O LAKES®** Butter, softened
- ¼ cup milk
- 1 teaspoon coconut extract or vanilla
- ½ cup sweetened flaked coconut, toasted

• Heat oven to 350°F. Grease and flour two (9-inch) round cake pans. Set aside.

• Combine cake mix, 1 cup water, banana and eggs in large bowl. Beat as directed on package. Stir in ¾ cup coconut by hand.

• Pour batter evenly into prepared pans. Bake for 30 to 35 minutes or until toothpick inserted in center comes out clean. Cool 10 minutes; remove from pans. (Run knife around side of pans before removing.) Cool completely.

• Meanwhile, combine 2 cups powdered sugar, butter, milk and extract in large bowl. Beat at medium speed, scraping bowl often, until creamy. Gradually add remaining powdered sugar, mixing until well blended.

• Place 1 cake layer onto serving plate; spread with ½ cup frosting. Cover with second cake layer; spread top and sides of cake with remaining frosting. Sprinkle with toasted coconut.

tip:

To toast coconut, spread coconut in single layer on ungreased baking sheet. Bake at 350°F., stirring occasionally, for 5 to 7 minutes or until lightly browned.

Creamy Lemon Pie with Berries

Preparation time: **15 minutes** | Baking time: **6 minutes** | **8 servings**

CRUST

- 1¼ cups graham cracker crumbs
- 6 tablespoons **LAND O LAKES®** Butter, melted
- ¼ cup sugar

FILLING

- 1 cup cold milk
- 1 (3.4-ounce) package instant lemon pudding and pie filling mix

- 1 cup **LAND O LAKES®** Sour Cream
- 2 to 3 teaspoons freshly grated lemon peel
- 1 cup **LAND O LAKES™** Heavy Whipping Cream
- 2 tablespoons powdered sugar

FRUIT

- 2 cups assorted fresh berries

• Heat oven to 375°F. Combine all crust ingredients in medium bowl. Press firmly onto bottom and up sides of ungreased 9-inch pie pan. Bake for 6 to 8 minutes or until set. Cool completely.

• Meanwhile, combine milk and pudding mix in medium bowl; beat with wire whisk until blended. Stir in sour cream and lemon peel. Set aside.

• Beat whipping cream in chilled small bowl at high speed, scraping bowl often, until soft peaks form. Continue beating, adding powdered sugar, until stiff peaks form (1 to 2 minutes).

• Gently stir 1 cup whipped cream into lemon mixture. Spoon mixture into crumb crust. Spread remaining whipped cream over lemon filling. Refrigerate until set (at least 2 hours).

• Combine fruit in medium bowl. To serve, cut pie into wedges; top with fruit.

Dairy Country Chocolate Sheet Cake

Preparation time: **30 minutes** | Baking time: **20 minutes** | **48 servings**

CAKE

- 1 cup **LAND O LAKES®** Butter
- 1 cup water
- ¼ cup unsweetened cocoa
- 2 cups all-purpose flour
- 2 cups sugar
- ½ teaspoon salt
- ½ cup **LAND O LAKES®** Sour Cream
- 2 eggs
- 1 teaspoon baking soda

FROSTING

- ½ cup **LAND O LAKES®** Butter
- ¼ cup unsweetened cocoa
- 6 tablespoons milk
- 3½ cups powdered sugar
- 1 cup chopped pecans
- 1 teaspoon vanilla

• Heat oven to 350°F. Combine 1 cup butter, water and ¼ cup cocoa in 3-quart saucepan. Cook over medium heat, stirring occasionally, until mixture comes to a boil (6 to 7 minutes). Remove pan from heat. Add flour, sugar and salt; mix well. Add sour cream, eggs and baking soda; beat until smooth.

• Spread batter into greased 15×10×1-inch jelly-roll pan. Bake for 20 to 22 minutes or until toothpick inserted in center comes out clean.

• Meanwhile, combine ½ cup butter, ¼ cup cocoa and milk in 2-quart saucepan. Cook over medium heat, stirring occasionally, until mixture comes to a boil (3 to 4 minutes).

• Remove from heat. Add powdered sugar; beat until well mixed. Stir in pecans and vanilla. Spread over warm cake.

Double Chocolate Snack Cake

Preparation time: **15 minutes** | Baking time: **35 minutes** | **9 servings**

1½ cups all-purpose flour
1 cup sugar
½ cup real semi-sweet
  chocolate chunks*
¼ cup unsweetened cocoa
1 teaspoon baking soda
½ teaspoon salt

⅓ cup **LAND O LAKES®** Butter,
  melted
1 tablespoon white vinegar
1 teaspoon vanilla
1 cup cold water

Powdered sugar, if desired

• Heat oven to 325°F. Combine flour, sugar, chocolate chunks, cocoa, baking soda and salt in ungreased 8-inch square baking dish. Make three depressions in flour mixture. Pour butter into one, vinegar into the second and vanilla into the third. Pour water over all ingredients; stir until well mixed.

• Bake for 35 to 40 minutes or until toothpick inserted in center comes out clean. Cool completely. Sprinkle with powdered sugar, if desired.

*Substitute ½ cup real semi-sweet chocolate chips.

tip:

To be sure that you are not overbaking your cake, set timer for the minimum time specified in the recipe. To test for doneness, simply insert a toothpick near the center of the cake. It should come out clean and dry. If it is wet and covered with batter, reset the timer for 2 more minutes, then retest.

Lime Pudding Cake

Preparation time: **20 minutes** | Baking time: **42 minutes** | **6 servings**

3 eggs, separated
1 cup sugar
⅓ cup **LAND O LAKES®** Butter, softened
¼ cup lime juice
1 tablespoon freshly grated lime peel
¼ cup all-purpose flour

⅛ teaspoon salt
1 cup fat-free skim milk

Powdered sugar, if desired
LAND O LAKES™ Heavy Whipping Cream, whipped, if desired
Grated lime peel, if desired

• Heat oven to 350°F. Beat egg whites in small bowl at high speed until foamy. Continue beating, gradually adding ¼ cup sugar, until glossy and stiff peaks form (2 to 3 minutes). Set aside.

• Combine remaining ¾ cup sugar and butter in large bowl. Beat at medium speed, scraping bowl often, until creamy. Add egg yolks, lime juice and 1 tablespoon lime peel; continue beating until well mixed. Add flour and salt; continue beating until well mixed. Stir in milk by hand. Gently stir in beaten egg whites.

• Pour mixture into ungreased 1½-quart casserole. Place casserole into 13×9-inch baking pan. Place baking pan on oven rack; pour boiling water into baking pan to ½-inch depth.

• Bake for 42 to 52 minutes or until golden brown. Remove from water; cool at least 30 minutes.

• To serve, sprinkle with powdered sugar, if desired. Garnish with whipped cream and grated lime peel, if desired.

Old-Fashioned Apple Crisp

Preparation time: **20 minutes** | Baking time: **25 minutes** | **6 servings**

6 medium (6 cups) apples,
   peeled, cored, sliced
¾ cup firmly packed brown
   sugar
¾ cup uncooked old-fashioned
   oats

½ cup all-purpose flour
1 teaspoon ground cinnamon
½ cup cold **LAND O LAKES®**
   Butter

Vanilla ice cream, if desired

• Heat oven to 375°F. Place apples into ungreased 9-inch square (2-quart) baking dish.

• Combine brown sugar, oats, flour and cinnamon in medium bowl; cut in butter with pastry blender or fork until mixture resembles coarse crumbs. Sprinkle sugar mixture over apples. Bake for 25 to 35 minutes or until apples are tender and topping is golden brown. Serve warm with ice cream, if desired.

tip:

Select an apple variety recommended for baking or use a combination of baking apples, such as Granny Smith, McIntosh and Braeburn.

Orange Sour Cream Poppy Seed Cake

Preparation time: **20 minutes** | Baking time: **45 minutes** | **9 servings**

CAKE

2 cups all-purpose flour
1 tablespoon poppy seed
1 teaspoon baking soda
½ teaspoon baking powder
½ teaspoon salt
1 cup sugar
½ cup **LAND O LAKES®** Butter, softened

1 cup **LAND O LAKES®** Sour Cream
1 egg
2 teaspoons freshly grated orange peel
⅓ cup orange juice

GLAZE

6 tablespoons powdered sugar
1 tablespoon orange juice

• Heat oven to 350°F. Stir together flour, poppy seed, baking soda, baking powder and salt in medium bowl; set aside.

• Combine sugar and butter in large bowl. Beat at medium speed, scraping bowl often, until creamy. Add sour cream, egg and orange peel. Continue beating, scraping bowl often, until well mixed. Reduce speed to low. Beat, gradually adding flour mixture alternately with orange juice and scraping bowl often, until well mixed.

• Spread into greased 8-inch square baking pan. Bake for 45 to 50 minutes or until toothpick inserted in center comes out clean.

• Meanwhile, stir together glaze ingredients in small bowl; drizzle over warm cake. Serve warm or cool.

S'More Pie

Preparation time: **30 minutes** | Baking time: **4 minutes** | **12 servings**

CRUST
- 1¼ cups (about 18) finely crushed graham crackers
- ¼ cup sugar
- ⅓ cup **LAND O LAKES®** Butter, melted

FILLING
- ⅔ cup **LAND O LAKES™** Heavy Whipping Cream
- 2 (7-ounce) milk chocolate candy bars, broken into pieces
- ½ teaspoon vanilla

TOPPING
- 1⅓ cups **LAND O LAKES™** Heavy Whipping Cream
- 1 cup marshmallow crème
- 2 (1.55-ounce) milk chocolate candy bars, broken into pieces

• Heat oven to 375°F. Combine all crust ingredients in medium bowl. Press onto bottom of ungreased 9-inch springform or pie pan. Bake for 4 to 5 minutes or until lightly browned. Cool completely.

• Meanwhile, heat ⅔ cup whipping cream in 1-quart saucepan over medium heat, stirring occasionally, until cream just comes to a boil (2 to 3 minutes). Remove from heat. Add all remaining filling ingredients; stir until smooth. Pour over cooled crust. Freeze 30 minutes.

• Combine 1⅓ cups whipping cream and marshmallow crème in large bowl. Beat at high speed until stiff peaks form. Spread over chocolate filling. Garnish with candy bar pieces. Refrigerate at least 4 hours or overnight.

Apricot-Raspberry Tart

Preparation time: **15 minutes** | Baking time: **38 minutes** | **8 servings**

CRUST
1 (9-inch) unbaked refrigerated pie crust

FILLING
1 (12.5-ounce) can almond filling
1 (15-ounce) can apricot halves, well-drained

1 (6-ounce) container (1 cup) fresh raspberries
1 tablespoon sugar

GARNISH
2 tablespoons apricot preserves
LAND O LAKES™ Heavy Whipping Cream, whipped, sweetened, if desired

• Heat oven to 400°F. Press crust onto bottom and up sides of ungreased 9-inch round or 11×7-inch tart pan with removable bottom. Bake for 8 minutes.

• Spread almond filling evenly into partially baked crust. Arrange apricots over filling; sprinkle with raspberries and 1 tablespoon sugar. Bake for 30 to 40 minutes or until crust is lightly browned. Cool completely.

• Place preserves in microwave-safe bowl. Microwave on HIGH for 15 to 30 seconds or until melted. Brush tart with melted preserves. Serve with whipped cream, if desired.

tip:

If canned almond filling is not available, make your own. Place 1 cup slivered almonds in food processor bowl fitted with metal blade. Cover; process until finely chopped. Add ¾ cup sugar, ¼ cup **LAND O LAKES®** Butter and 1 tablespoon all-purpose flour; process until well mixed. Add 1 egg, 2 tablespoons **LAND O LAKES™** Half & Half and 1 teaspoon almond extract. Cover; process until well mixed.

Raspberry Streusel Coffee Cake

Preparation time: **25 minutes** | Baking time: **45 minutes** | **12 servings**

COFFEE CAKE

- 2 cups all-purpose flour
- 1 teaspoon baking powder
- ½ teaspoon baking soda
- ¼ teaspoon salt
- ¾ cup sugar
- ½ cup **LAND O LAKES®** Butter, softened
- 2 eggs
- 1 teaspoon almond extract
- ¾ cup buttermilk*

- ½ cup seedless red raspberry preserves

TOPPING

- 3 tablespoons all-purpose flour
- 1 tablespoon sugar
- 2 tablespoons cold **LAND O LAKES®** Butter
- 3 tablespoons uncooked quick-cooking oats
- 3 tablespoons sliced almonds

• Heat oven to 350°F. Combine 2 cups flour, baking powder, baking soda and salt in medium bowl; set aside.

• Combine ¾ cup sugar and ½ cup butter in large bowl. Beat at medium speed, scraping bowl often, until creamy. Add eggs and almond extract; continue beating, scraping bowl often, until well mixed.

• Reduce speed to low. Beat, gradually adding flour mixture alternately with buttermilk, until well mixed. Spread batter into greased 9-inch springform pan. Spoon preserves over batter. Using spatula or knife, swirl preserves into batter.

• Combine 3 tablespoons flour and 1 tablespoon sugar in medium bowl; cut in 2 tablespoons cold butter with pastry blender or fork until mixture resembles coarse crumbs. Stir in oats and almonds. Sprinkle over batter.

• Bake for 45 to 50 minutes or until toothpick inserted in center comes out clean. Cool 10 minutes on wire rack; remove sides of pan.

*Substitute 2 teaspoons vinegar or lemon juice and enough milk to equal ¾ cup. Let stand 10 minutes.

Rhubarb Streusel Bread

Preparation time: 40 minutes | Baking time: **1 hour 5 minutes** | **12 servings**

BREAD

- 1 cup sugar
- ½ cup **LAND O LAKES®** Butter, softened
- ⅓ cup orange juice
- 2 eggs
- 2 cups all-purpose flour
- 1 teaspoon baking powder
- ¼ teaspoon baking soda
- ¼ teaspoon salt
- 1½ cups sliced ¼ -inch fresh rhubarb*

STREUSEL

- 2 tablespoons sugar
- 2 tablespoons firmly packed brown sugar
- 1 tablespoon all-purpose flour
- 1 tablespoon **LAND O LAKES®** Butter, melted
- 1½ teaspoons ground cinnamon

• Heat oven to 350°F. Grease and flour 8×4-inch loaf pan.

• Combine 1 cup sugar and ½ cup butter in large bowl. Beat at medium speed, scraping bowl often, until creamy. Reduce speed to low; add orange juice and eggs. Continue beating just until mixed. (Mixture will look slightly curdled.) Stir in flour, baking powder, baking soda and salt by hand just until moistened. Gently stir in rhubarb. (Batter will be thick.)

• Reserve 1½ cups batter. Spread remaining batter into prepared pan. Combine all streusel ingredients in small bowl; stir until mixture resembles coarse crumbs. Sprinkle half of streusel over batter in pan; gently press into batter. Carefully spread reserved batter into pan; top with remaining streusel. Press streusel into batter.

• Bake for 65 to 70 minutes or until toothpick inserted in center comes out clean. Cool 10 minutes; remove from pan.

*Substitute 1½ cups frozen rhubarb, thawed.

Coconut Cherry Scones with Citrus Butter

Preparation time: **20 minutes** | Baking time: **20 minutes** | **8 scones; ½ cup Citrus Butter**

CITRUS BUTTER

- ½ cup **LAND O LAKES®** Butter, softened
- 1 tablespoon powdered sugar
- 1 teaspoon freshly grated lemon peel
- 1 teaspoon freshly grated orange peel

SCONES

- 2 cups all-purpose flour
- ¼ cup sugar
- 2½ teaspoons baking powder
- ¼ teaspoon salt

- ½ cup cold **LAND O LAKES®** Butter
- 1 egg, beaten
- ½ cup **LAND O LAKES™** Half & Half
- ⅓ cup sweetened flaked coconut
- ½ cup dried cherries or sweetened dried cranberries, chopped
- 1 teaspoon freshly grated lemon peel
- 1 tablespoon coarse grain or decorator sugar

• Heat oven to 375°F. Combine all citrus butter ingredients in small bowl. Beat at low speed, scraping bowl often, until creamy. Set aside.

• Combine flour, sugar, baking powder and salt in medium bowl; cut in ½ cup butter with pastry blender or fork until mixture resembles coarse crumbs. Combine egg, half & half, coconut, cherries and lemon peel in small bowl. Add to flour mixture. Stir just until flour mixture is moistened.

• Turn dough onto lightly floured surface; knead lightly 8 to 10 times. Pat dough into 7-inch circle. Place onto greased baking sheet. Cut into 8 wedges. (Do not separate.) Sprinkle with coarse sugar. Bake for 20 to 25 minutes or until golden brown. Cool 15 minutes. Cut wedges apart; remove from baking sheet. Serve warm scones with Citrus Butter.

Nutmeg Streusel Muffins

Preparation time: **10 minutes** | Baking time: **18 minutes** | **1 dozen muffins**

STREUSEL

1⅓ cups all-purpose flour
1 cup firmly packed brown sugar
½ cup cold **LAND O LAKES®** Butter

MUFFINS

⅔ cup all-purpose flour
⅔ cup buttermilk*
1 egg
1½ teaspoons baking powder
1½ teaspoons ground nutmeg
½ teaspoon baking soda
½ teaspoon salt

• Heat oven to 400°F. Combine 1⅓ cups flour and brown sugar in large bowl; cut in butter with pastry blender or fork until mixture resembles coarse crumbs. Reserve ½ cup.

• Add all muffin ingredients to remaining streusel mixture in same bowl; stir just until moistened.

• Spoon batter into greased or paper-lined 12-cup muffin pan. Sprinkle each with reserved streusel. Bake for 18 to 22 minutes or until lightly browned. Let stand 5 minutes; remove from pan.

*Substitute 2 teaspoons vinegar or lemon juice and enough milk to equal ⅔ cup. Let stand 10 minutes.

Oat Bran Popovers with Herb Butter

Preparation time: **15 minutes** | Baking time: **35 minutes** | **6 popovers; ⅓ cup Herb Butter**

HERB BUTTER

- ⅓ cup **LAND O LAKES®** Butter, softened
- 1 teaspoon finely chopped fresh oregano leaves*
- 1 teaspoon chopped fresh parsley

POPOVERS

- 3 eggs
- 1¼ cups milk
- 1 tablespoon **LAND O LAKES®** Butter, melted
- 1 cup all-purpose flour
- ¼ cup oat bran
- ¼ teaspoon salt

• Heat oven to 450°F. Stir together ⅓ cup butter, oregano and parsley in small bowl. Cover; refrigerate until serving time.

• Beat eggs in small bowl at medium speed, scraping bowl often, until thick and lemon-colored. Add milk and 1 tablespoon butter; continue beating 1 minute. Add flour, oat bran and salt; continue beating until well mixed. Pour batter into well-greased popover pan or 6-ounce custard cups. Bake for 15 minutes.

• Reduce oven temperature to 350°F. (DO NOT OPEN OVEN DOOR.) Bake for 20 to 25 minutes or until golden brown.

• Insert knife into popovers to allow steam to escape. Serve immediately with Herb Butter.

*Substitute ½ teaspoon dried oregano leaves, crushed.

tip:

Eggs and milk should be at room temperature to help ensure successful popovers.

Orange Praline Quick Bread

Preparation time: **20 minutes** | Baking time: **30 minutes** | **32 servings (4 mini loaves)**

BREAD

1 cup sugar
1 cup **LAND O LAKES®** Sour Cream
½ cup **LAND O LAKES®** Butter, softened
2 eggs
1 tablespoon freshly grated orange peel
1 teaspoon vanilla
2 cups all-purpose flour

2 teaspoons baking powder
½ teaspoon baking soda
½ teaspoon salt
1 cup chopped pecans

GLAZE

⅓ cup firmly packed brown sugar
⅓ cup **LAND O LAKES®** Butter
¼ cup finely chopped pecans

• Heat oven to 350°F. Combine sugar, sour cream, butter, eggs, orange peel and vanilla in large bowl. Beat at medium speed, scraping bowl often, until well mixed. Reduce speed to low; add flour, baking powder, baking soda and salt. Beat just until moistened. Stir in 1 cup pecans.

• Spoon batter evenly into four greased 5½×3-inch mini-loaf pans. Bake for 30 to 35 minutes or until toothpick inserted in center comes out clean. Cool 10 minutes; remove from pans.

• Meanwhile, combine brown sugar and ⅓ cup butter in 1-quart saucepan. Cook over medium heat until mixture comes to a boil (3 to 4 minutes). Spoon glaze mixture over warm loaves. Immediately sprinkle with ¼ cup pecans.

tip:

Substitute one 9×5-inch greased loaf pan. Bake for 60 to 65 minutes.

Mini Poppy Seed Muffins

Preparation time: **25 minutes** | Baking time: **15 minutes** | **3 dozen mini muffins**

1⅓ cups all-purpose flour
2 tablespoons poppy seed
½ teaspoon baking powder
¼ teaspoon baking soda
⅛ teaspoon salt
¾ cup sugar
⅔ cup **LAND O LAKES®** Butter, softened

2 eggs
1 teaspoon vanilla
¼ teaspoon lemon extract, if desired
⅓ cup lemon yogurt

• Heat oven to 350°F. Line 36 mini muffin cups with paper liners. Combine flour, poppy seed, baking powder, baking soda and salt in medium bowl. Set aside.

• Combine sugar and butter in large bowl. Beat at medium speed, scraping bowl often, until creamy. Add eggs, one at a time, beating well after each addition. Add vanilla and lemon extract; mix well. Reduce speed to low; alternately add flour mixture and yogurt, beating after each addition, just until moistened.

• Spoon batter into prepared mini muffin cups. Bake for 15 to 18 minutes or until set and very lightly browned.

Apple-Nut Coffee Cake

Preparation time: **20 minutes** | Baking time: **30 minutes** | **15 servings**

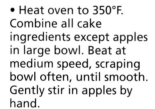

CAKE

2 cups all-purpose flour
1 cup sugar
½ cup **LAND O LAKES®** Sour Cream
½ cup **LAND O LAKES®** Butter, softened
¼ cup milk
2 eggs
1 teaspoon baking powder
1 teaspoon baking soda
1 teaspoon vanilla
¼ teaspoon salt
2 medium (2 cups) cooking apples, peeled, chopped*

TOPPING

½ cup chopped walnuts or pecans
½ cup firmly packed brown sugar
2 tablespoons **LAND O LAKES®** Butter, melted
1 teaspoon ground cinnamon

• Heat oven to 350°F. Combine all cake ingredients except apples in large bowl. Beat at medium speed, scraping bowl often, until smooth. Gently stir in apples by hand.

• Spread batter into greased 13×9-inch baking pan. Combine all topping ingredients in small bowl; sprinkle over batter.

• Bake for 30 to 35 minutes or until toothpick inserted in center comes out clean.

*Substitute 1 (16-ounce) can peaches, drained, chopped.

tip:

We recommend using Red Rome, Winesap, McIntosh or Haralson apples.

Banana Honey Muffins

Preparation time: **15 minutes** | Baking time: **28 minutes** | **18 muffins**

1½ cups bran cereal
¾ cup milk
½ cup **LAND O LAKES®** Butter, melted
⅓ cup honey
2 medium (1 cup) ripe bananas, mashed

1 egg, slightly beaten
1¼ cups all-purpose flour
1 tablespoon baking powder
½ teaspoon salt

1 tablespoon large-grain raw sugar

• Heat oven to 375°F. Stir together bran cereal and milk in large bowl. Let stand 5 minutes.

• Stir butter, honey, bananas and egg into bran cereal mixture. Stir in flour, baking powder and salt just until moistened.

• Spoon batter evenly into 18 paper-lined muffin cups. Sprinkle each muffin with raw sugar. Bake for 15 to 18 minutes or until lightly browned.

tip:

This recipe will yield 6 jumbo muffins. Bake for 28 to 32 minutes or until lightly browned.

Eggnog Muffins with Spiced Butter

Preparation time: **15 minutes** | Baking time: **20 minutes** | 1 dozen muffins

SPICED BUTTER
- ½ cup **LAND O LAKES®** Butter, softened
- 1 tablespoon powdered sugar
- ½ teaspoon ground cinnamon
- ¼ teaspoon ground nutmeg

MUFFINS
- 1 cup dairy or canned eggnog or **LAND O LAKES™** Fat Free Half & Half
- ¼ cup **LAND O LAKES®** Butter, melted
- 1 egg, slightly beaten

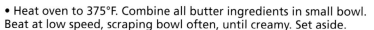

- 1 teaspoon rum extract
- 2 cups all-purpose flour
- ¼ cup sugar
- 2 teaspoons baking powder
- ½ teaspoon salt
- 1 teaspoon ground nutmeg

TOPPING
- ¼ cup sugar
- ½ teaspoon ground cinnamon
- ½ teaspoon ground nutmeg
- ¼ cup **LAND O LAKES®** Butter, melted

• Heat oven to 375°F. Combine all butter ingredients in small bowl. Beat at low speed, scraping bowl often, until creamy. Set aside.

• Combine eggnog, ¼ cup melted butter, egg and rum extract in large bowl. Add all remaining muffin ingredients; stir just until moistened.

• Spoon batter into greased or paper-lined 12-cup muffin pan. Bake for 20 to 25 minutes or until light brown. Cool slightly; remove from pan.

• Meanwhile, combine all topping ingredients except butter in small shallow bowl. Pour ¼ cup melted butter into another small bowl. Dip tops of muffins in melted butter, then in topping mixture. Serve warm with spiced butter.

Golden Pumpkin Bread

Preparation time: **30 minutes** | Baking time: **45 minutes** | **16 servings**

1½ cups all-purpose flour
1 cup firmly packed brown sugar
1 cup canned pumpkin
½ cup **LAND O LAKES®** Butter, softened
2 eggs

1½ teaspoons ground cinnamon
1 teaspoon baking powder
1 teaspoon baking soda
1 teaspoon salt
½ teaspoon ground ginger
¼ teaspoon ground cloves

• Heat oven to 350°F. Combine all ingredients in large bowl. Beat at medium speed, scraping bowl often, until well mixed.

• Spoon into greased 9×5-inch loaf pan. Bake for 45 to 55 minutes or until toothpick inserted in center comes out clean. Cool 10 minutes; remove from pan. Cool completely.

tip:

Substitute three greased 5½×3-inch mini loaf pans. Bake for 30 to 35 minutes or until toothpick inserted in center comes out clean.

Walnut Banana Bread

Preparation time: **15 minutes** | Baking time: **1 hour** | **16 servings**

¾ cup sugar
½ cup **LAND O LAKES®** Butter, softened
2 eggs
2 medium (1 cup) bananas, mashed

½ teaspoon vanilla
1½ cups all-purpose flour
1 cup chopped walnuts
½ teaspoon baking soda
½ teaspoon salt
¼ teaspoon ground cinnamon

• Heat oven to 350°F. Combine sugar and butter in large bowl. Beat at medium speed, scraping bowl often, until creamy. Add eggs; continue beating until well mixed. Reduce speed to low; add bananas and vanilla. Beat until well mixed. Stir in all remaining ingredients by hand.

• Spoon batter into greased and floured 8×4-inch loaf pan. Bake for 60 to 70 minutes or until toothpick inserted in center comes out clean. Let stand 10 minutes; remove from pan. Cool completely.

tip:

For easy slicing, wrap in plastic food wrap and refrigerate overnight. This allows the crust to soften.

Three-Grain Sunflower Muffins

Preparation time: **20 minutes** | Baking time: **15 minutes** | **12 muffins**

1 cup milk
½ cup **LAND O LAKES®** Butter, melted
1 egg
1½ cups all-purpose flour
½ cup cornmeal
½ cup uncooked old-fashioned oats

½ cup firmly packed brown sugar
¼ cup roasted shelled sunflower seeds
1 tablespoon baking powder
½ teaspoon salt
2 tablespoons roasted shelled sunflower seeds

• Heat oven to 400°F. Combine milk, melted butter and egg in large bowl with wire whisk.

• Combine flour, cornmeal, oats, brown sugar, ¼ cup sunflower seeds, baking powder and salt in medium bowl. Stir flour mixture into milk mixture just until moistened.

• Spoon batter evenly into greased or paper-lined 12-cup muffin pan. Sprinkle tops evenly with 2 tablespoons sunflower seeds. Bake for 15 to 18 minutes or until golden brown.

tip:

Seeds and nuts are packed with protein. You can use salted or unsalted sunflower seeds in this recipe.

Best-Loved Blueberry Muffins

Preparation time: **15 minutes** | Baking time: **22 minutes** | **1 dozen muffins**

MUFFINS

- 1 cup milk
- ½ cup **LAND O LAKES®** Butter, melted
- 1 egg, slightly beaten
- 2 cups all-purpose flour
- ⅓ cup sugar
- 2 teaspoons baking powder
- 1 teaspoon salt
- 1 cup fresh or frozen blueberries

TOPPING

- ¼ cup **LAND O LAKES®** Butter, melted
- ¼ cup sugar

• Heat oven to 375°F. Combine milk, ½ cup melted butter and egg in large bowl. Add all remaining muffin ingredients except blueberries; stir just until moistened. Gently stir in blueberries.

• Spoon batter into greased or paper-lined 12-cup muffin pan. Bake for 22 to 26 minutes or until golden brown. Cool slightly; remove from pan.

• Dip tops of muffins in ¼ cup melted butter, then in sugar.

variations:

Lemon Blueberry Muffins: Prepare muffins as directed, stirring in 1 tablespoon freshly grated lemon peel with flour. Bake as directed.

Raspberry-White Chocolate Chip Muffins: Omit blueberries. Add 1 cup fresh or frozen raspberries for blueberries. Gently stir in ½ cup white baking chips with raspberries.